How to Paint a Dead Man

poems by

Harry Bauld

Finishing Line Press
Georgetown, Kentucky

How to Paint a Dead Man

For Xabier

Para dibujar hay que cerrar los ojos y cantar. —Picasso

What terrifies us about death is not the loss of the future but the loss of the past —Kundera

I see the rorschach for the dead on its way —Berryman

Into the artifice of eternity —Yeats

Copyright © 2020 by Harry Bauld
ISBN 978-1-64662-351-8 First Edition
All rights reserved under International and Pan-American Copyright Conventions. No part of this book may be reproduced in any manner whatsoever without written permission from the publisher, except in the case of brief quotations embodied in critical articles and reviews.

ACKNOWLEDGMENTS

Many thanks to publications in which some poems first appeared.

Profit, *Sixfold*
Boxer, *Winning Writers*
A Reasonable Man, *Deliberately Thirsty* (UK)

Publisher: Leah Huete de Maines
Editor: Christen Kincaid
Cover Art: The Anatomy Lesson of Dr. Nicolaes Tulp by Rembrandt
Author Photo: Inés Gómez-Ochoa
Cover Design: Harry Bauld

Order online: www.finishinglinepress.com
also available on amazon.com

Author inquiries and mail orders:
Finishing Line Press
P. O. Box 1626
Georgetown, Kentucky 40324
U. S. A.

Table of Contents

The Eyes 1

Duals in the Old West 2

The Docent 4

I Drop Mark Strand into the Toilet at The Mansion 5

Revision 6

School 7

Majorities 9

Daniel Gravius in Zeeland 10

Magritte's Toilet 12

How to Paint a Dead Man 13

Table of Discontents 14

Middle Knowledge 15

Death Penalty 16

Profit 18

Last Days, Beautiful Days: A Widow's Story 19

Tangled Up in Blue 21

Boxer 23

Cadillac Moon 24

Annunciation 25

Self Portrait as Marco Polo as Miles Davis 26

Poison, Oasis 28

Me and You, Canaletto 29

Submission Guidelines 30

A Reasonable Man 31

The Eyes
Neue Gallery, Self Portraits, June 2019

Most of these Germans
scare the paint out of you, Felix Nussbaum
in the camp, a few bones

in the background and
another figure struggling up
from voiding in a trash can,

the sky dark with its human smoke.
Everyone's looking at you
except Max Beckmann. Otto Dix's

gaze is all Aryan accusation
but you do not confess. And he is
no Nazi. That is just you

soiling yourself. Your daughters
are Jewish. Keep repeating. Lovis Corinth

gives himself in the mirror another
mirror. Does he even have a good side?
Do we any longer?

Kirchner's garish
complementaries look forward—

to what, in that Germany? Always now
it seems we look at art and it looks back

at us on trial. Your daughters
are Jewish. Your gorge rises

against history. You are not getting anywhere
that way, seen and seeing and stuck. Enough.

Can't you take it? The gallery empties you
onto the same hot and sunny avenue

where the president says he can
shoot someone and not lose a vote.

1

Duals in the Old West

Art is always saying hello and poetry is always saying goodbye.
    —Kenneth Koch

Body is always saying yes and soul is always saying no.

Music is always saying you can fly and dance is always saying check out these glutes.

Sex is always saying put it in and money is always saying take it out.

History is always saying what's your name again? and the future is always saying guess what?

No idea what the present is saying.

Baseball is always saying wait and basketball is always saying now.

Eggs are always saying symmetry and bacon is always squealing discord.

Economics is always saying check please and psychology is always singing Irving Berlin's "What'll I Do."

Stonehenge is always saying you should get a piercing and the Parthenon is always saying there are other colors than black.

Fishing is always saying up and skiing is always saying down.

Books are always saying well done and the internet is always saying oops.

Studying is always saying stop and teaching is always saying go. And vice versa.

Windows are always saying go ahead and doors are always saying no way.

Movies are always saying gotcha and ads are always saying the same damn thing, over and over.

Yin is always saying yang and yang is always watching the game.

Churches are always saying too much and universities are always saying not enough.

Biology is always saying come in and chemistry is always saying get out.

Architecture is always saying always and drama is always saying never again.

Cities are always saying welcome and farms are always saying go away.

Jazz is always speaking French and country is always crying in its beer.

Novels are always saying where and essays are always saying how.

Eating is always saying glad to hear it and drinking is always saying sorry.

Philosophy is always saying ch ch ch changes and mathematics is always humming "Just the Way You Are."

The galaxy is always saying what can I get you? and black holes are always saying we're closed.

Spain is always saying ¿como que no? and New York is always saying excuse me, do you have the time or should I just go fuck myself?

Melody is always saying abracadabra and harmony is always saying fee fi fo fum.

Heat is always saying here and noise is always saying there.

Land is always saying war and water is always also saying war.

The Great Chain of Being is always saying we got this and secular humanism is always saying dunno.

Blacksmithing is always saying certainly and legerdemain is always saying doubt it.

The sun is always saying shut up and the moon is always whispering tell me more.

The surface is always saying why and depth is always saying because.

The Docent
Neue Gallery, New York

Something indecent
about her voice—too slow,

too loud, too parnassian, the
unctuous uplift as if she's teaching

iambic pentameter: "*with BED room
EYES and PARTed LIPS she LOOKS*

*as IF she FEELS roMANtic LOVE. Her FATHer
IS Klimt's DOCtor...*" Curlicued settees,

ancient marble, baroque mirrors,
the heartbeat of the recreated Viennese

drawing room down the street
from Nathan's hot dogs

and tourist *tchotchkes*, not such
a long shot from Freud. The woman

in gold. On gold. Gold gold
gold. Something here *is*

decadent. But the Nazis
did not destroy her; they saved it all,

like the judge condemning obscenity
who watches over and over

in his somber chambers the 8mm reel
of the woman and the horse

and preserves the evidence
just to be absolutely sure.

I Drop Mark Strand into the Toilet at The Mansion

Another poet told my daughter, his student,
"Don't sleep with him." Now in the diner on 86th
and York I'm reading *Blizzard of One* and in the decent
interval between sunnyside eggs (no toast) and green tea
I visit the john the little boys the men's the head WC
gents loo can privy latrine jakes khazi powder
room netty commode crapper and man
about a horse. Not wanting to leave Mark
stranded (sorry!) among the crumbs and sorry
congealings, I carry the slender hardcover which now
slips from its perch high atop the Pulitzer
down the almost-clean porcelain
slant I didn't notice atop the almost-clean tank. So many
others would have been better suited for this plunge—
any of the current infestation of invertebrates
in the Senate for one. *Into the Vortex of Crap
Dove the One Hundred!* But they're already locked
in an outhouse of their own making and here
is poor Mark Strand alone, newly dead, Clint Eastwood
look-alike, my daughter's prof. A Canadian!
His words drowning! Don't sleep
with him! Don't worry, he's dead!
An accident, of course, your honor—not his death
but his book falling into a toilet, like losing
bladder control with age, though since I have not
already released (praise be) the bowl is at least as clean
as it is going to get. Without thinking I reach
right in—Save Mark Strand!—seize him
by the jacket (too late!) anointed
with *eau de toilette* and shake
the leaves, just beginning to pleat, that tinkle
over the bowl—not the relief I was
looking for—then in the too too sullied
sink wash and wash my hands but of course
there are no paper towels to dry myself
of the drenching reek of poems.

Revision
    —Leda and the Swan, Georg Pencz, the Prado

It's she who seems to be the pet, still
leashed and nude, the gooseneck of god caressed
by the painter's stiff sable, the timid bill
for his meager services keeping barely abreast

of his monthly nut, and so the push
to strut his stuff. But. More than on her thighs,
he's lavished his limited gifts on the rush
of red velvet (fancy!) and a rag that lies

like an afterthought athwart the *mons* there,
her neck defective PVC, no tower
of ivory: the head on wrong.
                              Could she look up,
she'd see he's circled three birds in the air—
voyeurs, like those three kids, of art's power,
of which he knows he hasn't got a drop.

School

> *It is still the case that names are known of artists of that time who at present have no works credited to them. Who are these artists who are being dragged out from under the Master's enormous shadow?*
>   —Anthony Bailey, Responses to Rembrandt

He couldn't touch me
for lace, everyone knew

that. I conceded him
the darks; that's what

I came to see, colleague
but no follower. I wanted

to watch him do it. No harm
in that—the curious commerce

of teaching, the legitimate
theft. What you don't want

copied, you don't trot out
for all to see. The old man

was not stupid. Some of us,
Fabritius, Maes, Drost,

picked it up all right, layers
and layers of gloom that glowed

into light. Not for me
that kind of shadow,

it turned out. No magician
can do every trick.

He'd sell your stuff
right off the easel

if you let him—daub
some fur or flesh

or steel, sign his name
and boom, out the door

to feed the luxury habit,
the furniture, the models'

frippery and hats
for the juicy mistress.

But that wasn't
our deal. I had it

backwards on him. I was
the lace man. The faces

were his but bits
of the brushwork

in the collars, those little white
knots and frets and filigree

below the sitter's chin that lie
just fallen like prayer or

divine crumbs in the laps
of little angels, the ordinary

magic that makes a window
of the darkness and props up

the jaws of the prosperous—
every touch but the name was mine.

Majorities

> *Most poems....make no impression at all. They're like condoms on the beach.*
> —Garrison Keillor

Most critics....make no impression at all.
 They're like mink spit on the mattress.

Most introductions....make no impression at all.
 They're like sputum in the wisteria.

Most experts....make no impression at all.
 They're like tampons in the orange grove.

Most radio shows....make no impression at all.
 They're like crack vials in the Elysian fields.

Most macho males......make no impression at all.
 They're like guano on the bankside.

Most arguments....make no impression at all.
 They're like suppositories on an iceberg.

Most philistines....make no impression at all.
 They're like deer ticks in the batter's box.

Most politicians ....make no impression at all.
 They're like douche bags in the fjord.

Most judgments....make no impression at all.
 They're like bat farts in the history books.

Most tweets....make no impression at all.
 They're like enema bulbs on the glacier.

Most folksy appeals....make no impression at all.
 They're like ear wax in the bayou.

Most literary theories....make no impression at all.
 They're like smegma in the temple.

Daniel Gravius in Zeeland
1681

In Formosa I found no words
for gambling or servitude; here,

the grinding of microscope
and telescope, lenses on the far

and near. To Soulang I was only disciple
sent to preach the gospel

to that whole world
but no Messiah, never believed

the mission was only craft
and trade, unholy exchange

of Qing for Ming. Mine
was just a single word made flesh

and beyond. I was not that light,
but sent to bear witness

to a blinding and found
there are no synonyms.

Would I had not rendered
and so rent Matthew into a song
of Sinkang, tongue too pure

for the *shameful and odious
character* of we who governed

then and now in *Nederlandse*. In judgment
I sued superiors, was fined, reassigned,

retired to this middle burg among
the easy covenants, another wife

and life. Cattle I am not ashamed
to have brought the Siraya

into the service of God and cultivation.
Even then I knew: this was language

that cannot survive us,
a people of the flats like us

but too early, whose gods
raised the sediment of their rivers

to cure and conjure silt by their suns
into the hard indecent argil

of the omphalos, birth serpents
and the wide-eared heads

of those dark unbreakable
men and half-naked women

who stared like miners
and, like the words

of their low flat land,
will not be translated.

Magritte's Toilet

A chain hangs from the tank. My peen
aches, and a lousy crumbiness
in my pocket drains
my cents. Do I make or peep?

*I know what your hand
is doing in there* said the priest.

I yank the chain, I flush, let fall
upon the horns of still life,
I peed. As must have he. This window
was his transparent eyeball.

O window, you look just like your pictures!

A quiet house, not an umbrella nor sewing
machine stirring, let alone coupling on an operating
table. Attar of clouds. The bathtub yawns
sans torsos and pipes and vice versa.

When is a museum not
a museum? When it is a toilet in a museum,
the coolest tile where no one can live
anymore because it is a museum.

How many lightbulbs does it take
to change a surrealist? One apple,
mental, bowdlerized and besuited.
In the mirror my words are rightly reversed
but I am obversed and interdict, staring into the back

of my own back. Thank god the staircase
goes nowhere and the piano is a half step
out of town, I mean tune, towed
by priests. The poorly executed timing
of the bladder like a shower
of overcoats ticks me off and on.

How To Paint a Dead Man
The Craftsman's Handbook, Cennino Cennini, 1437

First you have to cut out all the stars with the ruler
sharpened like a pen or like your style,
your hand so unsteady that it will waver more
and flutter far more than leaves do in wind.

At the top, where structure is most spread out
and delicate, that is the best,
and this is indulging too much
in the company of women. Let us get back to our subject.

There is no keeping company with it.
Fling yourself on it and do not have too much respect,
for it fades in the open. Then blow quite hard into this opening
and look out for yourself. Beware of soiling your mouth with it.

Pick out the forms of the face as I showed
you for a wall. The handsome man must
be swarthy or horny from the tinting
mixture and so, while you are laying the first coat,

remedy this. You must know what bone
is good. Not being so strong, it is just as if
you were fasting. The whole man is eight
faces. Those of a woman I will disregard.

You may also get a stone. How? Put in some clear
warm water. The slabs must be clean.
Shape the star on it, ray by ray,
and let us suppose that in a day

you have just one head to do. Go back
to working up or grinding, then wait
a day or so. Bear this well in mind
and you will end by gaining your ambition.

Table of Discontents

The Wailing No One Asked For	1
Mewling Suet and Cruel Gruel	5
Wens and Buboes, Pustules and Pubes	6
Hormonic Infrequency	11
Addled Less Sense	17
Work In and Out of Progress: Rages and Pages	28
A Matterhorn of Dark Matter	45
Universitatis Vanitatum	73
Disappearance of Frogs and Cartilage	118
Mishits and Wounds	191
The FU Fugue	309
Cooking for Children	500
Infinity Won't Leave Us Alone	809
Why Am I Not Taller?	1309
Tennis without the Internet	2118
Epilogue of Losses	3427

Middle Knowledge
Death: Current Perspectives, Edwin Shneidman 1976

Even though it occurs only at the far end
of life, one of the most impressive facts
about death today is middle knowledge,
a definite break with living. To know
the facts is desirable. A family in Greece
sent a relative to the hospital to get
well; however, he died. Such fluctuations
imply *great uncertainties about length of life.*

Many successes are failures
in disguise. You die
from *something*—an unjustifiable
violation, a marathon task undertaken
by the recorder. This is a view
of the nature of man which identifies
his essence with the flowing of fluids
in the animal species, a lie which perhaps
soothed the survivors, but it is not true.

            When we say that a man has died,
there are appropriate behavioral changes.
Definitions of time, mode and shape of trajectory come later.
To describe the ghetto, the blockade, the scorched earth,
the famine, to suffer that skeleton I felt
a peculiar shudder—half thrill and half fright:

The terminal phase is about to begin.
Just as soon as this bleeding stops
(or the wound heals, or this infection
clears up) I'll be on my way.

Death Penalty

A father is no longer (if he once was)
         a father when he lies
                  On Jan. 6, 2017, a shooter opened fire
dead on twelfth night or whenever you will. A few others
         (who might as well be everyone else, again)
have just been shot in the airport by Ms. Santiago's hijo. This is statistics.
                 Five people were killed
     Numbers spring into action.
              another eight wounded.
Your father lying in the Ft. Lauderdale hospital
              at a baggage carousel at Fort Lauderdale-
              Hollywood International Airport
has a number you can't remember, toe-tagged and no longer waiting
            People scrambled
and you are 1000 miles away typing frsyj nr mpy [tpif.
              to grab their luggage—and find
     Helicopters swarm. Police lock down
              their loved ones. Some families were separated

the hospital. Your father does not speak Spanish. He has not been
              in the chaos; several parents were
shot. Florida, from the Spanish, "full of flowers"
              separated from their children during
              the commotion
or "red faced,"
              Broward Sheriff Scott Israel wouldn't name
              the victims or disclose their genders or ages.
or both. The Spanish brought disease that knocked off most of the Tequesta
              No motive was revealed
and now your father, though you don't blame the Spanish,
too busy with their jamon and nuns and cigarettes and olives and grapes
     and guitars and their own fascist legacy and present paro
              In August 2018, a federal judge sentenced
              Esteban Santiago to life
to have a role in this passing. Though your own wife is Basque
     your Spanish is ragged as a shot pattern. He has been tagged
by natural forces too various to name but not number. What he once was
              in prison
stiffens with wait. The dead in lockdown require no waiters.
              He had no intention of escaping
These are the stats of rage and triage, though your father

        He had pleaded guilty to the airport killings
who left when you were eighteen
   also does not speak French or no longer if he ever did,
something else you don't know and never did
     and never will. His old roar lies
numb to the lyric of sirens, those shrilling waiters,
    dumb to the disappearance of some number of others whose sum
you are waiting to hear along with all the departing frogs and caddisflies
that signal this earth our warming tomb. Other waiters,
       He couldn't elaborate on
his sister and a second wife hum their dirge and wait
        the extent of the injuries suffered
six hours in lockdown beside one who has ceased
        by the wounded, all of whom are being treated
        at area hospitals
his aging, for once progressing cleanly
    through the fresh stages: "Autolysis and the Acids: A Biography"
with ruptured cell pellicles leading to a slow pallor
    taking the edge off the living floridization of the flesh
       The shooter surrendered to police
     without a struggle
that once flailed through tempests of spirits now gliding
    soberly through its flowerless rigors. His revels now are ended,
his first wife, your mother, already vanished into air, into thick air,
       Passengers and airport personnel panicked
and his spirit, like the baseless fabric of a mass shooter's vision
   has dissolved and leaves not a rack of lamb or liquor behind,
       about an hour after the shooting
like that point in your own backward and abysm of time from him
       when a second gunman was falsely reported
     at the airport
forty years estranged, which used to turn like a page but now is pegged
   like old mucilage, the gunk childhood's learning smells like.
More than a sum sung of pasts, tomorrow is a mortification
   waiting in an unknown tongue.

Profit
    —*Basquiat, 1982*

In the tic tac toe of this space, what year will it be
when time arrows itself into your late rally?

One blue hole in the punctured ozone of downtown
is all the sky you get in this economy.

Eenie meenie miney moe, catch a market by the toe,
out goes you and your bloody trellis of halo.

Tomorrow avoids your blackboard algorithms, mad matrix
of debt figured in the subway's antipodes.

This scream through the drain of teeth
we've heard before in a major, northern key.

Chase it, get it, spend it, because you know
something's running you down, something's coming;

even if you don't know what it is, you've seen
its panicked fingers bony in their bright ecstasies

erected into the only light left. You know
the position. Now turn it to your own ends.

Last Days, Beautiful Days: A Widow's Story
 —*a cento for Joyce Carol Oates*

1. Night-side

Big mouth and ugly girl, I lock my door
upon myself because it is bitter and because
it is my heart. You must remember this,
my sister, my love, naughty cherie,
I am no one you know: black girl/white girl,
black dahlia, white rose, mudwoman,
black water soul at the white heat,
broke heart blues—
a fair maiden missing Mom,
marriages and infidelities, unholy
loves, anonymous sins. Unusual suspects:
the gravedigger's daughter,
the tattooed girl, the accursed blonde, the doll master,
the assassins, beasts: expensive people, them.

2. Soul/Mate

Dear husband, Daddy Love, first love, time traveler,
Jack of Spades, angel of light, son of the morning,
the man without a shadow, lovely,
dark, deep—where are you going,
where have you been? Will you always
love me? Give me your heart, do with me what you will,
collector of hearts. Two or three things I forgot
to tell you: a) we were the Mulvaneys,
a bloodsmoor romance, sexy, sexy chix (double delight)
b) freaky green eyes what I lived for,
snake eyes—the faith of a writer, the truth teller,
the profane art, small avalanches,
the wheel of love, the rise of life on earth
c) where I've been and where I'm going:
high lonesome sourland in rough country,
telling stories: the hungry ghosts,
the fabulous beasts, George Bellows, the virgin
in the rose bower, the bingo master, the woman
who laughed, the goddess, the perfectionist, Marya
the rescuer, the lamb of Abyssalia

and other women, women whose lives
are food, men whose lives
are money—all the good people
I've left behind, the sacrifice after the wreck. I picked
myself up, the female of the species,
spread my wings, and flew away, man crazy
little bird of heaven.

3. Where is Here?

Hudson river, the falls, Carthage,
the barrens, the lost landscape, devil's half acre
upon the sweeping flood by the north gate,
a garden of earthly delights, the temple
in the region of ice—contraries, tone clusters, the edge
of impossibility: I'll take you there
in darkest America. You can't catch me
crossing the border. Hang on
to your own bone dreaming America
with shuddering fall, love and its derangements,
zombie American appetites, a book
of American martyrs. My heart laid bare,
Starr Bright will be with you soon.

Tangled Up in Blue
> *Those trying to explain pictures are as a rule completely mistaken.*
> —Picasso on Art, 1972

Color? I don't know. Yes, no, yes. Maybe.
Blue—what does blue mean?
Women, women, women.
Why do two colors, put one next to the other, sing?
How often haven't I found that,
wanting to use a blue, I didn't have it
so I used a red instead. The red
I took away from one place
turns up somewhere else. Color
weakens. What we impose upon ourselves
does not emanate from ourselves.
You think you aren't alone.
We make things for somebody.

You can talk of a steak
being blue when you mean red.
If you don't know what color to take,
take black.

It is not necessary
to use many words.
I want to say the nude
but succeed in *saying*
women, women, women.
That's what I want. You want two breasts?
Well, here you are—two breasts.

The arts are all the same,
x number of times, the same thing.
What is necessary is to name things.
I name the eye
I name the foot
I name my dog's head on someone's knees.
I name the knees:
women, women, women.

All this has been pure literature
not to say nonsense, and there you are
again, in chains.

The head is a very odd thing.
Look at these eyes.
They are deep holes cut into the wall.
For months I looked at the sideboard
without thinking more than "It's a sideboard."
To name. That's all. That's enough.

Boxer
—for Agha Shahid Ali, 1949-2001

I want to learn to sing with my hands,
To birth in the rest of me something to bring with my hands.

A drummer's hammer toward melody is one knuckle of it,
No rest in that furious offering with my hands.

Each shot rattles the gums behind the mouthpiece,
Head voice that jabs language I sign with my hands,

Cast up with my deaf breath in the barn where I train
Like a magic coin I pretend to fling with my hands.

Each word, each digit deserves it's own toll,
Even in forms whose necks I wring with my hands.

Does this beat, once made, stalk the streets,
A prisoner I have set free, sprung with my hands?

I'd rather be water or dumb metal
Than bone that I, my own gravedigger, sling with my hands.

To practice so long for so little is to plant in dust
Gestures history may or may not ring with my hands

Taped, these pickers and stealers of multiple breaks
That reach out to you, to cling with my hands

To the broken distance between us. There isn't time
To pause, only feint, so I must think with my hands

And put down combinations, marks I make
On you in lines I string with my hands.

I am not another Ali, neither dancer nor dance, butterfly nor bee;
This, the only way I know to sing with my hands.

Cadillac Moon
    Basquiat, 1981

The car can't turn over more than a single vowel
ignition stuttering while it gathers for lift off
and works up to the long movie scream
of effort, the rend and let 'er rip of
Aaaaaaaaaaaaaaaaaaaaaaaaaaaaaaaaaaaaaaa
to leave off hanging in chains
and depart the chassis of ground
for the smudge of moon and the rising fall
of the scratchy A440 of the street

This is the ecstasy of flight
that can be drawn if not done
painted if not sung
the changes of somewhere over the black rainbow
that begin seared in the ascent
turning dusk and shadow as the cow of a sedan
almost clears the moon. This is not the same old
samo of anything ever assembled
along Mr. Ford's anti-semite line
but a set of fantasy wheels
that play like four square in the hands
of children who like the seven artists
who will save us, plow their fingers in paint furrows
to change all the colors of today's sky
rubbing out the authoritarian moon and everything under it
making a holy mess and moving on

Annunciation
   Angel, Basquiat, 1982

I'm here to tell you
and I know you're not asking
I told you once
a couple thousand years ago
but you couldn't hear
and don't have a choice now
because here I am again
the face of your own deaf self
dumb to your own glories
but I have to dish and go
a gig to play with a band of angels
in a light you can't look at
rounds to put in the bank
in a championship bout
you can't even see
so can't wait around for you

Boo! Go on
get yourself together
you better back up
box your own corner
because you already
gave birth to this flame
you don't know the name of

and *now* you want salvation?
come and get me
nothing to wait for
both of us coming apart
at the seams.

Self Portrait as Marco Polo as Miles Davis as Mr. Death
Basquiat, Untitled triptych, 1983

1.
Anatomy fiddles while jazz burns
four skulls in the old masters mausoleum.
Fie on this year's plaster cast and the atelier
of whomsoever, all the dead-drawn
masks. I'm the bird chowing down koko puffs
on a slow boat to China to bring the syncopation of spaghetti
back west to the sanatorium at Camarillo, to kick with my own feet,
eat the new word, feed the body clean and dark,
crown the beat just like that,
show you where everything is
in case you need to reconstruct, as who doesn't,
just let me show you my etchings in my study
and studio, *yo studio que pasa*. All my parts
press down and pop up like trumpet valves,
the three theaters of the body
rising up in hieroglyphic storm
of bone gone lean as line
like no kind of blue you ever knew—
when I was in shape the old trainer said
man, you look like a natomy chart
and now I just keep moving left, stick stick stick
and I measure your ass and every other piece of you
till I get into your China.
Punish the body and the head die
how that particular solo goes
and cost you something on those feet
to circle left all the way out
to the fifteenth round of the new world, baby.

2.

*My six year old nephew could do that,
a few crayons and a list of words
and some scribbles and stick figures.*

Sure he could, if he was the child God
making up the universe again from scratch.

3.
It's what you do after you go down
that counts. Jack Johnson,
his hand over his eyes with Willard
that slow white clod over him and the sun
burning the cloudless Havana sky,
and you can take your time working your way
down that image, one knee raised
and the truth on its back reflecting
maybe next time I get up.
The fix was in.
That next time is now
in this body laid out like the Black Ajax
melting in that Havana sun,
no wild child then, he doesn't
speak enough Spanish
to call the whole thing off,
his future and ours one moment unclear
and sold, singing *What did I do
to be so black and blue,*
so do we just have to go down,
and take a count, melting, melting,
all our beautiful wickedness
in the blue crown on our copyrighted skulls?

Poison, Oasis
    Acque Pericolose, Basquiat, 1981

Go on, Walt Whitman, get to the desert
if you dare and become
undisguised and naked *there*
till it chars your pink ass black as lightning
and then we'll talk. Out here's not like cruising
ye ole isle of Manhattoes
for sailors, I tell you that—
you want to bring your blackest halo
to light your way through the buffalo bones
and jump the hood-eye rattlers
playing their greeny blues at your feet
and gnats big as your face
nipping at your nuts.

                                Then you'll have to grant
you never saw authentic Sioux
(though you love them
yeah, yeah yeah) who'd put
an arrow in your white ass
soon as say *Kemosabi*. You've got, like,
one tree out here. No where to go
but when they finish burning
the planet down a hundred years
it'll be all the garden we have left. Better cover up,
this place is on fire and this patch of water
just pushes the venom through you faster
and paints your old grey head yellow
as a New York night
and swallows your blab, so if you want *me*,
want to look for *me*, grab onto those ribs
toasted in the sun and slide on under
but I tell you right now
inside those bones aint no kinda shade.

Me and You, Canaletto

Go fishing for the right color
Of summer clouds over the wet reek
Of these ancient domes. Here,
For example: thumbs of ash
In the temple of sky, very like
Whatever animal smut our polluted leaders
Dream up. This is our art, a something-scape,
Not what we want to render but it must do—
One moment of clouds blown across our windows
Like the dream balloon of our impermanence
Here in a canal-town fifth-floor walk-up
Turned neither to smoke nor water
But some purified smatter
With its own square in my periodic table
Beside the other muck, Canaletto,
I'm made of: soot, psalm, marrow.

Submission Guidelines

1. Please familiarize yourself with samples in dust and ashes.

2. Do not attach sleights, spells, cloaks, or ale.

3. You agree to quake and dole, bash and mar, try to abide, be capable of disturbing above and below the mark.

4. In the case of excess or violation the price will be liberty and roar.

5. After payment, do not clash or change.

6. Include the exact temporary address of at least one circle of hell, a seventeen-word biography in a language that hunts with the old weapons.

7. Disqualifications: too blue, insufficient admission, the word *shillelagh*, a single missing demon.

8. Multiple cringing is permitted with notification of ridicule and penury elsewhere.

9. Dislocation is encouraged but not required; harrowing, preferred.

10. If dying mothers appear in more than one location, judges must be notified.

11. These are the only guidelines.

12. By signing below you accept the terms of obligation in every conceivable way.

A Reasonable Man
 —William Morris, "The Aims of Art," 1887

A little trickle of water, a wheel, and a few
simple contrivances to carve the handle of his knife
leave him free to smoke his pipe and think,
to weave plain cloth, the little extra art
in the cloth, as long as he was free.

This I say in the teeth, something at present unnamed,
undreamed of: a reasonable man with a feeling for art
will only use it when he is forced to. And now
I must drop. I am unhappy indeed and almost wish
myself dead though I do not know what that means.

Some men are so directly without any metaphor at all
from a cathedral to a porridge-pot.
The poor devils of our own country side
and of our own slums, ignorant fisher-peasants,
half-mad monks, scatter-brained sansculottes
cannot even guess what it is to be dead.

I do not think that anything will take
the place of art though they hunt it about the world
so hard. It lies between stark utilitarianism,
a genuine interest in all the details of daily life,
and idiotic sham, the little rift within the lute.

Like the pre-historic men of the drift
we may find ourselves in a world blank and bare
that has accidentally some beauty about it,
consequences of old resistance to those curses—
starvation, overwork, dirt, ignorance, brutality.

On the other hand, it may lead us into the desert,
the lying dreams of history, this gibbering ghost
of the real thing; that is to say, if the thing were to go on
the earth's surface will be hideous everywhere
scratching forms of animals on their cleaned blade-bones.

Why does a reasonable man use a machine?
Partly for the sake of the hope.

Notes

"The Eyes" is for Inés Gomez-Ochoa

"I Drop Mark Strand into the Toilet at The Mansion" is for Elizabeth Straus. Mark Strand (1934-2014) won the Pulitzer Prize for poetry in 1999.

"Profit; Cadillac Moon; Annunciation; Self Portrait as Marco Polo as Miles Davis as Mr. Death; Poison, Oasis." Jean Michel Basquiat, 1980's artist of Haitian and Puerto Rican descent whose work began in street art and graffiti and transmuted into semi-abstract expressionist paintings of social commentary founded in be-bop and early hip hop, and which challenged systemic racism, colonialism, and existing structures of wealth and power, died of a heroin overdose in 1988 at the age of twenty-seven. In 2017, an untitled 1982 Basquiat sold at auction for 110.5 million, then a record for an American artist.

Jack Johnson (1878-1946). The first African-American heavyweight boxing champion held the title from 1908-1915. Many thought Johnson "took a dive" when he lost to Jess Willard in Havana in 1915 after winning almost every round, one piece of evidence for which is the photo of Johnson on his back in the 26th round actively shielding his eyes from the Cuban sun.

Jazz genius Miles Davis (1926-1991) was also, throughout his career, a painter.

"Death Penalty." Harold A. Bauld, 1930-2018

"Table of Discontents" is for Rick Somma

"Daniel Gravius in Zeeland." A Dutch missionary to Formosa, now Taiwan, Gravius (1616—1681) translated portions of the Bible into the native Siraya language. He ran afoul of Dutch authorities but eventually was completely exonerated and returned to his native Netherlands.

"Last Days, Beautiful Days: A Widow's Story." Poem composed entirely of the complete titles of books by Joyce Carol Oates, author of nearly sixty novels and counting, including some under two different pseudonyms, as well as a stack of volumes of short stories, poetry, plays, criticism, essays and other non-fiction. An apocryphal but persuasive anecdote of her astonishingly prolific creativity tells of a spectator at an Oates reading approaching her afterward. "I noticed you doing something with your hand on the podium while you were reading aloud," said the spectator. "I was writing another story," she replied.

Harry Bauld graduated from Medford High School in Massachusetts and studied art history at Columbia University where he was twice All-Ivy shortstop and broke Lou Gehrig's records. Unfortunately they were his academic records. As a freelance journalist for New England Monthly, Boston Magazine, People, and many others whose circulation he helped reduce almost to the vanishing point, his beats included the arts, sports, wine and spirits, and book reviews. He is the author of a previous poetry collection, The Uncorrected Eye (Passager Books) as well as a classic prose how-to guide based on his work as an admissions officer at Columbia and Brown, On Writing the College Application Essay (HarperCollins). His work has appeared in many journals and anthologies, won the New Millennium Writings Award, the Milton Kessler Poetry Prize, been nominated for a Pushcart Prize, and was selected by Matthew Dickman for inclusion in Best New Poets 2012 (University of Virginia Press). He has taught English and coached baseball, boxing and basketball at high schools in New York and New England. He has twice been honored as a Distinguished Teacher by the White House Commission on Presidential Scholars and currently teaches at Horace Mann in the Bronx.

www.ingramcontent.com/pod-product-compliance
Lightning Source LLC
LaVergne TN
LVHW040117080426
835507LV00041B/1234